Questions and Answers About
THE TRAIL OF TEARS

BRIANNA BATTISTA

PowerKiDS press.

NEW YORK

Published in 2019 by The Rosen Publishing Group, Inc.
29 East 21st Street, New York, NY 10010

First Edition

Editor: Brianna Battista
Book Design: Michael Flynn

Photo Credits: Cover Woolaroc Museum, Bartlesville, Oklahoma; cover, pp. 1, 3–12, 14–32 NuConcept Dezine/Shutterstock.com; p. 4 Silver Spiral Arts/Shutterstock.com; p. 5 © North Wind Picture Archives/Alamy; pp. 7, 13, 16, 27, 28, 29 courtesy of the Library of Congress; p. 9 (Washington) https://commons.wikimedia.org/wiki/File:Gilbert_Stuart_-_George_Washington_-_Google_Art_Project.jpg; p. 9 (letter) Library of Congress Manuscript Division, George Washington Papers collection; pp. 11, 15, 19, 23 National Archives and Records Administration; p. 14 Kean Collection/Archive Photos/Getty Images; p. 17 Newberry Library, Chicago, Illinois, USA/Bridgeman Images; p. 20 Library of Congress American Memory, A Century of Lawmaking for a New Nation online collection; p. 21 http://fortwiki.com/File:Fort_Marr_Blockhouse.jpg; p. 25 National Park Service.

Cataloging-in-Publication Data

Names: Battista, Brianna.
Title: Questions and answers about the Trail of Tears / Brianna Battista.
Description: New York : PowerKids Press, 2019. | Series: Eye on historical sources | Includes glossary and index.
Identifiers: LCCN ISBN 9781538341285 (pbk.) | ISBN 9781538341278 (library bound) | ISBN 9781538341292 (6 pack)
Subjects: LCSH: Trail of Tears, 1838-1839–Juvenile literature. | Indians of North America–Southern States--Relocation–Juvenile literature. | Cherokee Indians–History–Juvenile literature. | Cherokee Indians–Relocation--Juvenile literature.
Classification: LCC E99.C5 B325 2019 | DDC 975.004'97557–dc23

Manufactured in the United States of America

CPSIA Compliance Information: Batch #CS18PK: For Further Information contact Rosen Publishing, New York, New York at 1-800-237-9932

CONTENTS

WHO WERE THE CHEROKEES?

Before the arrival of European colonists, the Cherokees were one of the major Native American groups living in North America. The Cherokees had an advanced civilization and were known for being skilled hunters and fierce warriors. They grew crops, wove baskets, and used stone tools. The Cherokees were able to continue their way of life well into the eighteenth century while European colonists settled the land along the Atlantic coast.

CHEROKEE HANDWOVEN BASKET

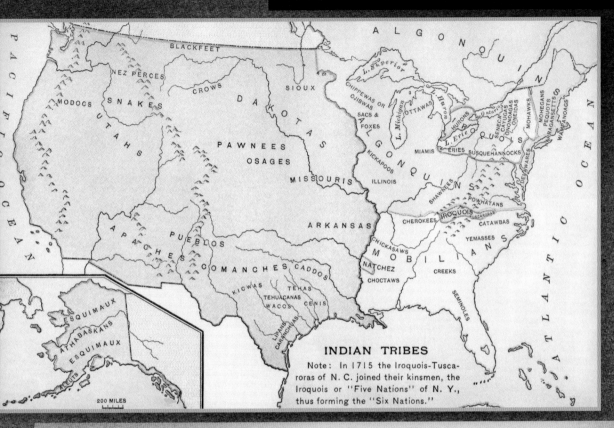

INDIAN TRIBES

Note: In 1715 the Iroquois-Tuscaroras of N. C. joined their kinsmen, the Iroquois or "Five Nations" of N. Y., thus forming the "Six Nations."

The Cherokee lands covered 135,000 square miles (349,648 sq km) from Georgia to Virginia. To the Native Americans, this land was sacred. It had been their home for a very long time and was the burial place of their loved ones. Their land was not to be sectioned out for individuals—it belonged to everyone.

5

INCOMING COLONISTS

When the first Europeans came to North America, they settled mostly along the Atlantic Coast. Throughout the eighteenth century, the populations of the coastal settlements grew, and the settlers moved inland. As they pushed farther west, away from the coast, the settlers began to move onto Cherokee land. They chopped down trees, built up homes, and began to hunt and farm on what they thought was unused territory.

These lands, however, were actually the hunting grounds of the Cherokees and other Native American groups. The Cherokees' attempts to protect their land often ended in bloody fights at the edges of their territory. Still, the settlers kept coming. They took over land that had belonged to the Cherokees for centuries.

AROUND 1901, W. L. WILLIAMS PAINTED WHAT HE BELIEVED LIFE IN PLYMOUTH, MASSACHUSETTS, WAS LIKE IN 1622.

Sources from the Past

Primary sources are works of writing or art that were created during the time period being studied. This painting isn't a primary source because it was painted nearly 300 years after the time it shows. Can we still learn anything about what life was like for the early settlers in North America by studying this painting? Would a painting from the early 1600s provide different or better information?

THE FIRST TREATY

The Cherokees soon grew angry about their land being taken by the American settlers. They protested to the government, and in 1785, the United States signed the Treaty of Hopewell with the Cherokees. This agreement made clear boundaries separating Cherokee land from the territory that was open for settlement. The treaty promised that the Cherokees would be protected by the government of the United States.

Enforcing this law, however, was difficult. Settlers chose not to honor the treaty and continued to take over the Native Americans' land. The Cherokees asked for help from President George Washington. Washington wrote back that he strongly wished to enforce the treaty. He asked the Senate for suggestions on how to solve the problem. More than 500 white families had moved onto Cherokee land.

To the Senate relative to the Cherokee nation of Indians.

United States August 11th 1790
Gentlemen of the Senate,

Although the treaty with the Creeks may be regarded as the main foundation of the future peace and prosperity of the South-western frontier of the United States, yet in order fully to effect so desirable an object the treaties which have been entered into with the other tribes in that quarter must be faithfully performed on our parts.

During the last year I laid before the Senate a particular statement of the case of the Cherokees— By a reference to that paper it will appear that the United States formed a treaty with the Cherokees in November 1785. That the said Cherokees thereby placed themselves under the protection of the United States and had a boundary assigned them.

That the white people settled on the frontiers had openly violated the said boundary by encroaching on the Indian Lands.

That the United States in Congress assembled did on the first day of September 1788 issue their proclamation forbidding such unwarrant: able

THIS IS THE LETTER PRESIDENT GEORGE WASHINGTON SENT TO THE SENATE. HE WAS CONCERNED THAT THE SETTLERS WEREN'T HONORING THE TREATY OF HOPEWELL.

TRY, TRY AGAIN

Instead of enforcing the Treaty of Hopewell and removing the white settlers, the Senate put a new treaty in place. In 1791, the Treaty of Holston was signed. The Cherokees gave up the land occupied by the settlers, and the government agreed to pay them $1,000 a year for the property.

Once again, however, the treaty failed to work. White families continued to cross the borders. The Cherokees protested again and again. In response, new treaties were made—and again broken. Each time another treaty was signed, more Cherokee land was given away to white settlers. The U.S. government paid the Cherokee nation for the land, but Cherokee hunting grounds were still getting smaller. The Cherokees were being forced farther and farther west.

Sources from the Past

Letters can be primary sources. Thomas Jefferson wrote his private letter to Congress on January 18, 1803, during a time of great unrest between Native Americans and white settlers who were moving onto their land. In his letter, Jefferson makes it clear that he wants the Native Americans off the land. What else can we learn about this period in history by studying Jefferson's letter?

Confidential.

Gentlemen of the Senate and of the House of Representatives.

As the continuance of the Act for establishing trading houses with the Indian tribes will be under the consideration of the legislature at it's present sefsion, I think it my duty to communicate the views which have guided me in the execution of that act; in order that you may decide on the policy of continuing it, in the present or any other form, or to discontinue it altogether if that shall, on the whole, seem most for the public good.

The Indian tribes residing within the limits of the US. have for a considerable time been growing more & more uneasy at the constant diminution of the territory they occupy, altho' effected by their own voluntary sales: and the policy has long been gaining strength with them of refusing absolutely, all further sale on any conditions. insomuch that, at this time, it hazards their friendship, and excites dangerous jealousies & perturbations in their minds to make any overture for the purchase of the smallest portions of their land. a very few tribes only are not yet obstinately in these dispositions. In order peaceably to counteract this policy of theirs, and to provide an extension of territory which the rapid increase of our numbers will call for, two measures are deemed expedient. First, to encourage them to abandon hunting, to apply to the raising stock, to agriculture and domestic manufacture, and thereby prove to themselves that lefs land & labour will maintain them in this, better than in their former mode of living. the extensive forests necefsary in the hunting life, will then become uselefs, & they will see advantage in exchanging them for the means of improving their farms, & of increasing their domestic comforts. Secondly to multiply trading houses among them, & place within their reach those things which will contribute more to their domestic comfort than the pofsefsion of extensive, but uncultivated wilds. experience & reflection will develope to them the wisdom of exchanging what they can spare & we want, for what we can spare and they want. in leading them thus to agriculture, to

11

FROM FRIENDSHIP TO BETRAYAL

Andrew Jackson was a general in the Tennessee **militia**. His first encounter with the Cherokees occurred when the two nations—the United States and the Cherokee—became **allies** in the Creek War (1813–1814). A group of Creeks known as the Red Sticks had vowed to kill all white settlers. The Cherokees, as well as Creeks who wanted peace, fought alongside the United States.

Without his Native American allies, Jackson probably wouldn't have won the final battle, the Battle of Horseshoe Bend. Without their help, the general might not have even survived the fight. Jackson had assured the Cherokees and other Native American groups that they were worthy of friendship in the eyes of the United States and that peace would be lasting.

ANDREW JACKSON WAS A GENERAL IN THE CREEK WAR AND BECAME ALLIES WITH THE CHEROKEE NATION.

The Cherokees believed a deep friendship had been formed and that Jackson would protect their interests. However, when the terms to end the war came out, the Native Americans were shocked. Jackson wanted 23 million acres (9.3 million ha) of land. Of this land, the Cherokees believed they owned 4 million acres (1.6 million ha). The Native Americans took their complaints to President James Madison, who urged Jackson to try to purchase the land through treaties instead.

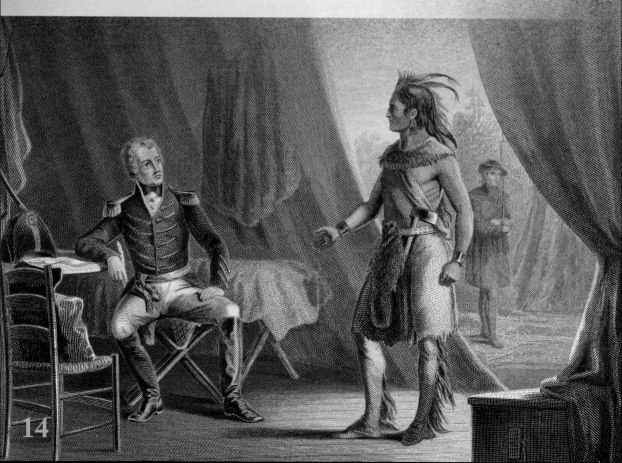

Jackson was mad and felt he'd rightfully won the land through battle. For a time, the Native Americans refused to sell their land to him. In the end, however, nine Cherokee chiefs signed the 1816 Treaty of Turkeytown, which gave the United States 1.3 million acres (526,091 ha) of land.

A NEW SURVIVAL APPROACH

Treaties kept being made, and they were becoming increasingly worse for the Native Americans. Many white Americans felt the Native Americans needed to be moved to the "Great American Desert" beyond the Mississippi River. This was because of their hunger for Native American land, but also fear. A number of popular books and newspapers told made-up stories of Native Americans doing terrible acts such as kidnapping women and children.

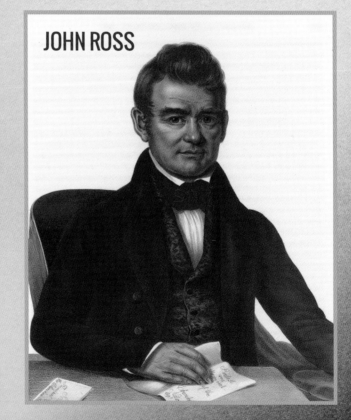

JOHN ROSS

THIS IMAGE FROM 1832 SHOWS NATIVE AMERICANS CAPTURING WHITE SETTLERS. IT WAS A COMMON, **RACIST** PRACTICE AT THIS TIME TO SHOW NATIVE AMERICANS BEHAVING IN TERRIBLE WAYS THAT WEREN'T ALWAYS TRUE.

The Cherokees knew the U.S. government wouldn't protect them. In 1827, the Cherokees drew up a **constitution**, elected John Ross to serve as principal chief, and stated they were their own separate nation. They set up a government similar to that of the United States. The Cherokees were doing their best to prove they should be taken seriously as a nation.

THE INDIAN REMOVAL ACT

In 1829, just as **tensions** were reaching their peak between Native Americans and white settlers, Andrew Jackson became president. Jackson may have seemed interested in land, but he actually had other plans. He believed Native Americans were **inferior** to white settlers, and he wanted to rid the United States of Native Americans completely.

In 1830, Jackson pushed the Indian Removal Act through Congress. This act gave the president the authority to give land west of the Mississippi River to Native American groups in exchange for the land they occupied. This was different from any previous Native American treaty in that there was no agreement between the two parties—it was an order.

IN 1830, PRESIDENT ANDREW JACKSON SENT A MESSAGE TO CONGRESS STRONGLY URGING IT TO APPROVE THE FORCED REMOVAL OF ALL NATIVE AMERICANS TO LANDS WEST OF THE MISSISSIPPI RIVER.

of the Indians beyond the white settlements,
is approaching to a happy consummation.
Two important tribes have accepted the
provision made for their removal at the last
session of Congress; and it is believed that
their example will induce the remaining
tribes, also, to seek the same obvious ad-
-vantages.

The consequences of a speedy re-
-moval will be important to the United
States, to individual States, and to the
Indians, themselves. The pecuniary ad-
-vantages which it promises to the govern-
-ment, are the least of its recommendations.
It puts an end to all possible danger of

Within weeks after Jackson was elected, the state of Georgia voted in favor of a bill that stripped the power from earlier Cherokee laws and treaties. Cherokee land was divided up, and white settlers started moving in. The Cherokees turned to the Supreme Court. After two court cases, the Court ruled that they weren't a different nation but a "distinct [special] community" that should be protected.

THE INDIAN REMOVAL ACT GAVE PRESIDENT JACKSON EXACTLY WHAT HE WANTED—ALL NATIVE AMERICAN LANDS EAST OF THE MISSISSIPPI RIVER.

President Jackson didn't enforce this ruling and actively worked against it with the Indian Removal Act. The Cherokees protested, and their elected principal chief, John Ross, tried to talk Jackson into any arrangement other than removal. But Jackson wouldn't budge. Five months after the act was signed, U.S. soldiers began building forts throughout Cherokee territory to lock up the Native Americans before they were moved west.

THE TREATY OF NEW ECHOTA

A small group of Cherokees began to think that agreeing to Jackson's wishes might be the only way to prevent the **destruction** of the entire nation. On December 29, 1835, twenty members of this Cherokee group gathered to sign the Treaty of New Echota, which would officially give up the land. The Native Americans would only have two years from the day the treaty became law to move west by choice.

The majority of the Cherokees felt **betrayed**. About 14,000 stood by Chief Ross, vowing to never leave their territory. For two years, Ross continued to write letters, take trips to Washington, and make appeal after appeal. However, his efforts proved unsuccessful when 7,000 U.S. soldiers arrived on Cherokee territory in May 1838.

purpose as soon after the ratification of this Treaty as an appropriation for the same shall be made. It is however not intended in this Article to interfere with that part of the Annuities due the Cherokees west by the Treaty of 1819

Article 19 This treaty after the same shall be ratified by the President & senate of the United States shall be obligatory on the Contracting parties.

In testimony whereof the Commissioners and the Chiefs head men & people whose names are hereunto annexed being duly authorized by the people in general Council assembled have affixed their hands & seals for themselves & in behalf of the Cherokee Nation. I have examined the foregoing treaty and altho' not present when it was made, I approve its provisions generally and therefore sign it.

Cae te hee his mark [Seal]   Wm Carroll [Seal]

Te gah e ska his mark [Seal]   J. F. Schermerhorn [Seal]

Robert Rogers [Seal]   Mayor his X Ridge mark [Seal]

John Gunter [Seal]   James his X Foster mark [Seal]

John A. Bell [Seal]   Tesa Taesky his X mark [Seal]

Charles F. Foreman [Seal]   Charles his X Moore mark [Seal]

William Rogers [Seal]   George his X Chambers mark [Seal]

George W Adair [Seal]   Tah yeske his X mark [Seal]

Elias Boudinot [Seal]   Archilla his X Smith mark [Seal]

James his X mark Starr [Seal]   Andrew Ross [Seal]

Jesse Halfbreed his X mark [Seal]   William Lasley [Seal]

Sources from the Past

Official government writings, such as the Treaty of New Echota, are considered primary sources. They give us proof of government activities and policies. Here we can see the names of the 20 Cherokees who signed the treaty against the wishes of the rest of the Cherokee nation. What else can we learn by studying this treaty?

A SAD JOURNEY

In May and June of 1838, the Cherokees who remained on their land were dragged from their homes and forced into crowded forts. Most weren't given time to gather any supplies or anything they owned. The U.S. soldiers attacked some of the Native Americans, though all weapons had been taken from the Cherokees.

The Native Americans who were forced west experienced great pain and misery, especially those who left in the late summer. Thousands of Cherokees had no blankets, and many had no shoes. People were dying because they didn't have enough food. As many as 20 Cherokees died each night due to sickness. Many who could no longer find the strength to continue walking simply sat by the side of the trail and waited for death to come.

THE CHEROKEES TRAVELED ALONG SEVERAL DIFFERENT ROUTES. TOGETHER THESE ROUTES BECAME KNOWN AS THE TRAIL OF TEARS. THIS NAME COMES FROM THE CHEROKEE NAME FOR THE JOURNEY: *DUNATLOHILVSTANVI*—"THE TRAIL WHERE THEY CRIED."

Sources from the Past

This map from the National Park Service is not a primary source. It was created in 2009, more than 150 years after Native Americans walked the Trail of Tears. Do you think this map is still a valuable source of information about the Trail of Tears? Why or why not?

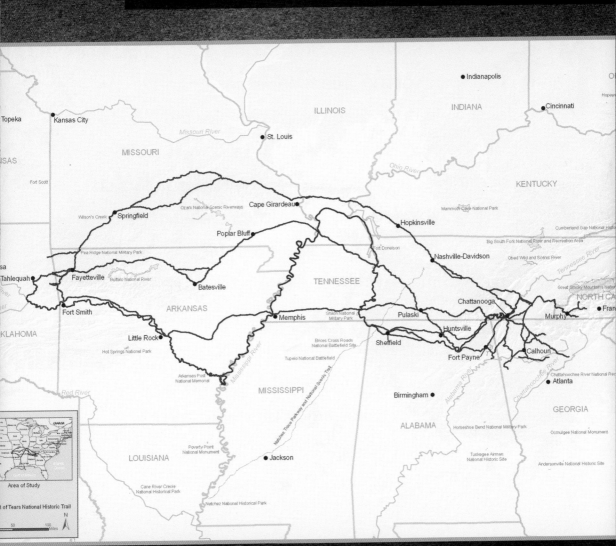

LIFE OUT WEST

The Cherokee people finally arrived in their new home out west. Along the way, they left around 4,000 unmarked graves—the result of too little food, exposure to the elements, and illnesses. Life wasn't easy for the Cherokees in their new home. Those who had moved west earlier already had their ways established. They weren't thrilled about sharing their land and **resources** with newcomers.

Conflict between the two groups—the Western Cherokees and the newcomer Eastern Cherokees— became bloody. Eventually, however, they realized they had to join together for the Cherokee nation to survive. They made a new plan and even created a new constitution together. They built schools, houses, roads, and businesses. At last, it seemed, the Cherokee people were at peace again.

OUT WEST, THE CHEROKEES MADE GREAT EFFORTS TO REBUILD THEIR NATION. PICTURED HERE IS THE CHEROKEE NATIONAL CAPITOL BUILDING IN TAHLEQUAH, THE CHEROKEE'S NEW CAPITAL CITY IN OKLAHOMA TERRITORY.

Sources from the Past

The Cherokee National Capitol Building was built in 1869. This early picture shows some of the original features of the building. The picture isn't dated, and is actually a copy of the original. Do you think this picture is a primary source? Why or why not? What can we learn about the Cherokee nation from this image without knowing the date of the original picture?

CHEROKEES IN THE CIVIL WAR

This period of peace and success didn't last long. The **American Civil War** soon drove a wedge through the Cherokee nation, with Cherokees fighting for both the North and the South. Between the Civil War battles and the additional battles that raged through Oklahoma, the Cherokees lost as much as one-third of their already decreased population.

THIS 1886 CARTOON OF THE CHEROKEE NATION SHOWS THE VARIOUS INTERESTS THAT WORKED TO DIVIDE THE CHEROKEE PEOPLE AND PUSH THEM OFF THEIR LANDS.

After the confusion of the Civil War, the westward movement of the United States' white population continued. Old treaties between the Cherokees and the United States were again broken, and new treaties were imposed upon the Cherokees. The Cherokees had more and more land taken away from them so railroads could be built. The expanding white population continued to spread into and settle on western lands.

THE NATION LIVES ON

By 1880, more whites lived in the Indian Territory set aside by the federal government than Native Americans. In 1887, the Dawes Act required that Cherokee land be split up among individual Cherokees, which again divided the Cherokee nation. The Curtis Act, passed in 1895, forced the Cherokees to **dissolve** their government. White settlers continued to take land from the Cherokees, and the Cherokee nation was officially dissolved on March 3, 1906.

The Cherokees became citizens of the new state of Oklahoma. Still, they held on to their **identity** as Cherokees and organized themselves as a nation again in 1938. Despite the history of lies and battles that it endured at the hands of the U.S. government, the Cherokee nation has survived and continues to stand tall with pride and strength today.

GLOSSARY

ally: One of two or more people or groups who work together.

American Civil War: A war fought from 1861 to 1865 between the North and the South in the United States over slavery and other issues.

betray: To hurt someone who trusts you by not giving help or doing something that is wrong.

constitution: The basic laws by which a country, state, or group is governed.

destruction: The state of being ruined.

dissolve: To break down completely.

enforce: To make sure people do what is required by a law or rule.

identity: The qualities and beliefs that make a person or a group different from others.

inferior: Less than or worse than something else.

militia: A group of people who are not an official part of the armed forces of a country but are trained like soldiers.

racist: Someone who believes that one group or race of people is better than another group or race.

resource: Something that can be used.

tension: A state in which people, groups, or countries disagree with and feel anger toward each other.

INDEX

WEBSITES

Due to the changing nature of Internet links, PowerKids Press has developed an online list of websites related to the subject of this book. This site is updated regularly. Please use this link to access the list: www.powerkidslinks.com/eohs/trail